We Sleep On Oyster Beds
By James White

Cover by Brenna Cumming and James White.

Published February 11th, 2018.
All Rights Reserved Copyright 2018.

Dedicated To

My love, my companion, my best friend, my Abbigayle. Without you, I would not have pushed myself as strong as I have. Your constant encouragement and criticisms, our running dialogues can not be thanked enough. My gratitude for you is in the blackheads you pick at, my cellphone gallery filled with candids of you, and what I see when I close my eyes. Thank you my Abbigayle. This book is dedicated to you and only you.

Part 1: Nature

The Last Hope Of Whitman Part 1

awnings rubbled
burying trunks in trenches

gate-hinge humful closing

doppler powered aircrafts;
lovecraftian overlords
over thine thin lord

party-fouls of another variety
perfumigation of debacchus
punchbowl spiked with mayweather rain

speckled peckers of mockingbird
of simmer-summer sway
of van-dyke champagne

bushels of amber-coated bees
fruiting upon oaken branch canopy
dwelling in cartoon casket potting
adrift upon pontoon of melted okra refuge

nepotism sneers nose-up in payolas of snootery
as bootlegged bottles be downed
as racket-bought rattletraps entrap no catfish today
on the dead-end sea where fish breath deadened black
where entombed pelagic plankton inkcrust pelicana
                                      of pontchartrain

boondocks of heron-legged youth
chasing the grecian frogger
hassling the po-man's newspaper ink for wallet-wads

freeks toss shekels at the those
who-are who-are
swaddled in mother's sky colored sundress
& daddy's pleather bootstrap

12-12 FL OZ CANS (144 FL OZ)
mouths dismembered cardboard
from toothy torn lips

listening to listerine gasoline gargles
of those outback in tubber facedown
drinking clear upchucked stomache

hampers of hamstrung cargo-briefs
sog in wrinkled panini-cloth of soak

fog fumes out two-bit industrial
as 8-bit haircuts spit-slosh,
spit the spiteful bitten uvula.

ulcered sacrosanct spoon-feed pigeons
used plastic-forks.
they gut out
dry-freeze backstrap wrapped in
pepper-gristle honeyslather.

bluebirds & dragonflies
loiter empty parking-lots
of foreclosed parks
to cranial chagrin

our end due to ne'er do wells.

our end due to never doing well
by another.

<u>All Of Us Earth</u>
slackjaw tendrils encroaching upon underbush of
        runting soil, brown in vulvine pure,
                minnows mellow in toady tombs,
while desperates attempt to dispirit this land away,

        unmanned menaces mow nothing
for the grass will outlive our blades,
shall emasculate the metal of malice
and accept its nutritional corpse with love,
        hamstringing it into honeybaked ham,

process of processing powers, produce sprouts uneaten
in vegetated alleyway caskets of raccoon foliage.

crippled clouding showers fog
the wet white of deadened dew
of spirit risings: ghostly goddesses each morning.

honey geysers out in pounds of pollen,
crossbreeding kingdoms of yellow,
amber platooning from lackadaisical depths,
hell birthing out life beautiful life beatific.

beastial green, heavenly skyward swayed to blue,
blood bleeds for and of you
and you and you and only you.
    swaddling your children in butterfly blankets,
lighting the streets: fireflies and glowworms,
clothing us in pelted hide and silkworm spittle,
gametean gods of game theory,
wormatozoa krakatoa in every crack of us.

we are nature unnatural.
monetary men of madness whom
kills and culls and cries for a home
that never left.

The Golden Calf Standard
cows behind fences
giving steel-eyed stares
at half past 12

nestling on mouth-mowed grass
propped beside another
with yellow plastic earrings
with water troughs in dirt
with passing cars as entertainment
with joggers as conversation
with a fence to bolster morale

Outback Backed Out

slabs of mid-morning matilda
of bushman rugged,
a nepal mountain range ribcage
jutting from noir skin;
crumbling nose wrinkled past its peak.
smiling in mockery of wind
trying to thieve your bundle.
sun bestilling your shoeless gnarl,
gnatted & scabbed.
beasts jumping to hip to feel
your caring caress,
pets of nurture so unnatural.
unambiguously animus,
enormous in that rural abnueral.
aborigine deity. conquest of time.
your beard wilted like spanish moss;
decayed shrub of whitman's snow-white skull.
your walks less frequent;
beasts have reverted back
into primordial marrow.
you have become pebbles
skipped on creekly lagoon
blue & green
by invisible younglings

Tastes Like Popeyes
martians
of marshland
clutch
chipped rocks
snug upon
splintering
mangrove knee hilts.

behind the head
they pierced
grassy leather pelt.

dinner, brunch,
boots, belts,
necklaces,
purses,
backscratchers,
paperweight,

(meanwhile dummy coyotes
only ever ate the meat).

yellow shuttles
carried us
offspring off to
the gator farm.

vats of swarming reptiles
on all sides
of the brown tiled walkway.

my friend Jaclyn
nervously asked the guide,
*what do
you feed them?*

he joked,
*there's a reason
they taste like chicken*

The Ant Queen Vociferi

anteater following the breadcrumb trail,
the 10 mile trenches of 6-legged grub,
rushing back to the queen of all ants,
mother-fuhrer of the kingdom of caverns,
tributes in tow to her throne
where the youngling make offerings
of meats, leaves, and honeydew

her gown of pelted anteaters embroidered
with mosquito & dragonfly wings;
her crown bejeweled with the slaughtered
queen bees preserved in amber,
pointed with pruned purple stingers of wasps

the anteater paralyzed and drug to chamber
by 20,000 scouters, the queen awaiting her guest.

her bolt-cutter mandibles squeeze into
the red-oak walls;
gushes of white syrup froth
into her silver goblet.

*"The wood eats termites spawned from their
imprisoned tyrant,"*
spoke the queen.

force-fed more gulps than breaths, white
viscous became the blood & sweat of the beast.

drowned in a glaze &
skinned for her new overcoat.

winter nears & spring melt will flood
her caverns as always, those trenches as always,

but the queen is warm

& her soldiers will be well-fed tonight;
feasting upon the sweet meat of giant.

Heron Dream
Grey bamboo stilts
coated in sky plumage
dusted in praline mud.

    A body of gatorskin
    when shaved,

jokes my grandpa,

dinosauria ancestral.

Our binocular eyes
gaze from
the deer-stand;
lining up shots
at heron heart,
at mackerel gut.

Winged shoulder scrawn
weak to copper slugs of
trigger-happy poachers
all too happy to kill
Our Great Blue.

Orange strikes the marsh
the way one spears stingrays
in clear water.

The Great Blue
takes off &
we love its leave.

Grandpa Jim nudges me,
pointing to a woodpecker
perched upon
a cypress knee.

No Land in NOLA

summer drawn to an end again;
silhouettes hit pavement
earlier each night.

ferries fewer &
fewer
plucked from midsummer nights
sunken on inland coves,
detoured by traffic-cones
orange in bonfire glow.

mardi gras floats
float amongst
a leaving levee.

purple beads tied to chopped down oaks
of Audubon to keep rafts stationed.

wreckage of Mark Twain's Pizzeria
breeching on off-occasions.

neckless rats floating on priceless paintings
eating our pearl necklaces
the way children once ate purple beads.

<u>The Last Hope Of Whitman Part 2</u>
the beginning is the morning worming;
simpsonian sunshine dancing that 5 AM martyrdom.

Mordecai in a stickshift Pontiac
drugracing a
1963 Buick Riviera
along riverland stretch
of dryconderoga swelter

roadside cherry-trees bud
blossoms of stork hearts,
mice eyes, & sickly amsinckia

kingfish/pins troll aging acreage of peach-pits
forever festering into fertilizer
for earthen quarries

ghostly zygote atop vertebral babels;
delta-delphi mystikós lost in mist hazed
uninitiated.

con-men calling themselves conservationists;
conversationalist schmoozers.
boozers roughing-up roofied snoozers
without a modicum of guilt.
polo wearing wantons of unwanted grope.
maximizing on maxwells till they are unwell
& hazed into a freshman-sized death.

beggared aristocrat utters

    "the goodwill to power
    rules us all"

    "overalls & chipped-monk skulls
    make streets shine pagan
    make needy need less
    make weeds wander poleward
    seeking a more temperate climate"

Shucks

A plucked mollusk shucked
into two brown rocky leaves
locked by ligament;

it puddles with BP blood,

its pearl a sheep eye,

pupil and petrol
equally black.

chucked
into the trash can
penitentiary
with the others,

an ink lagoon
of inedible.

Springtime In Aokigahara

In March my branches
entangle with rope;

discards of idle bones

remnants of weary necks.

The mink and bats leave
nothing more than soft hairs
& chipped teeth.

Hinoki cypress
only ever bloom
black belts of vine.

I bud envy for the forests
who scarf
only the wool
of a forgotten picnic getaway
for I am all too nauseated
with the taste of
jettisoned citizenry
& the staled slag of Fuji.

<u>Canyon of Bones</u>
Vertical cliff
hidden in mist

Grandmother said
a temple
of spirits
lives amongst
your high moss.

On my own in
this canyon
I eat charcoal
and venison.

I dream of an
ocean rising higher
than the cliffs

Flooding this dwelling
with green moss and
flowerlike spirits

The fall waterfall
uproots burnt oak
and terracotta pottery.

I wake up
licked by rain
beside the
ruined warmth
of smolder.

On the freshly skinned pelt
resided a charcoal drawing
of a resting face.

Tangipahoa Parish
a flat of strawberries
a lake of lazing bovines
a stringer of dead sac-a-lait
a barge of sunbathing chairs
a swamp of mosquito eggs
a liter of brown bag
a river of red kayaks
a roadside of boar skulls
a pathway of quartz pebbles
a riverbank of buzzards

mice eat
the noses off of
taxidermied bucks

pumpkin patches
grow gourds

railroad spike ladders
rise into
the bow stand

old shingles
fashioned out of
recycled coke cans
and milk cartons

poachers harvest
moccasin eggs-
scrambling them
in an empty shell
of a golden brown
box turtle

april showers cool
hairless alpacas
fenced in beside
mountains
of separated silt

Animal Kingdom

The Prince Mongoose
arrived in his dining room;
his servants and family and guests
awaiting his return.

Platters of
garden-snake
spaghetti
and baked goose
smothering white
embroidered linens.

"God Bless Acetylcholine!"
they cheered in squeaky jubilee
before downing
their fang milked wine.

After dinner
two Cobras
fought to the death
for their entertainment
in the chateau.

Drunk;
they spoke
of the Ant Queen

spoke of public opinion

spoke of her termite queen captive

spoke of their ally the Anteater King
and the pressures of his citizenry

spoke of a pre-emptive strike

spoke of firebombing
her fire-ants
and her rumored
mountain of gold

spoke of her
billion mindless captives
working to her whims
in desperate need of saviors.

The Last Hope Of Whitman Part 3

foothills only a feet high
a   m i l e   l o n g w a r d

neo-confederate clydesdales
clomp-clomp
pentagram clovers
into moldy mulch
into feldspar superglue.

beer-goggles only
block *vapor~wave~lengths*
of the victor's block party neon.

my grandfather's collection of still-lifes
were nothing but zoom-death.

self-awareness: an allusionary friend,
a mask worn-
down during staring contests
with empty sprucewood medicine cabinet;
reflectionless glow of anullysis,
of useless ulysses.

blooms of leopold
with leopard-print petals;
an advertisers wet dream.
river of liquor pebbles,
liquefied gold,
liquid assets of sweatshop sweat,
liquid incentive of sweatshirts half-off,
liquid incense of canned
church candles.

red solo cups of coupons
scissored by those
who view savings
as their savior.

mascarpone scented tulips
blossoming from buzzard beak.

like to think you found happiness
but you probably think you don't deserve that.

the selfless are selfish with their hate.

shampoo made of watery dentures
cleanses only mildew molars.

a burp in my fucking face
of shower-water,

& I am infinitely in love.

Part 2: Human Nature

The Last Hope Of Whitman Part 4
this dwelling is a perfect cube

unearth its cinderblock base
you'll find concrete coffin.

its parasites purr for validation.

"if only it were that easy."
"if only i were that easy."
stutters drunken wine-breath.

hidden guilt
riddles them with paranoia.

gallons of soybean sobbings
keep the canines soothed.

"shush brain shush," says woman wandering late at
hushed dusk on a bike-trail near Biloxi,

cramped boots
crushing the mushroom glow

room mushing into relaxation
each breath a sigh of existence
a gasp of fleeting
a fleeting few have survived.

"apologize to the blown out candles;
& bleached out smocks of red!"
he speaks to herself.

"feed me something better"
the starving boy says.

beggars can be choosers
when worshipping broken down beings,
when flag-burnings & book burnings are
the only warmth found most nights.

To Heaven And Back

Young men paddle down thinned Mississippi
garnishing in white-knuckled grasps
the feminist femurs of their shipman Enron;

        a clenched moccasin neck
that killed their daughters unborn,
guiding the voyage.

Wafts of watered-down firewater forest airways
in unbreathable savory:
potent as aged-pink-lemonade.

Ball-gowns, with circumferences wider than
umbrella, litter soaked porches that flatline
with termite screams
when stray cats ponder a paw upon wood
in search of burrowed whiskers within those
                        paled garment-nesting.

Garden-beds weep wet rose-petals
& oil-teethed pelicans grimace
  half as wide as the dead alligator boots.

Docked-to-harbor with an unused noose
:a lasso   of lost:
2 men land upon a motherland of frosted fog
          nostrilling up her duchess dirt;

                            they call out
without an echo of "welcome home""".

Street-corner tombstones of Lafayette
                          and Iberville
    Bonaparte   and Aquinas
    rise out   like rusted wheezing weeds;

pigeons stuffed upon picayune and beignets,
    murmuring their chainsmoker jabber;

the men respond in tongues-less sighs.

Outreached branches of cemetery-floor
  like zombie panhandlers of pity;

shovels dishevel cloudful dirt
of distant relatives.

"*All gold is fool's gold*" sighs the shovels,
but the young men are selectively deaf.

they untie their noose and leave it for another.

their tincan canoe sinks like Icarus.

their daughters' halos float like inner-tubes.

An Encyclopedia About Japan
    I.
pastures of idling wasabi;
ricing shores of thinned tsunamis;

4-fingered fathers give shinai kisses
to shins of their kindred children.

    II.
nation of riceless rations and raceless ashes;

shinto shrines stripped into
bamboo splints for splintered skeletal.

the rising sol; now but a sinking shingetsu.

    III.
shipping containers of rolling green;
yakuza klansmen jacuzzi each sunset motel;

mahjong parlors of rīchi hands
with shanghai shingles marbled on like soy sauce.

    IV.
convenience store men gawk at manga while
mini-skirt kimonos pass without catcall acknowledgement.

unmarried marios with yoshi body-pillows & luigi lungs;

shuttles sardine their sardonic suit carcasses.

    V.
vr virus versus an ever-ceasing us.

u.s. markets quick to capitalize upon
uncared for NEETS, those killed by Karōshi,
& a country whose tongue tires of microwave sushi.

Friends Of The Street Poets
fresh off the bus
without a dollar or job;
moved into fiance's flat.
you two only met once but
been long distance for years.
you speak & think
like a younger version of my cousin
---

got guitar on your back
tar in your hair
a piano-key smile
a kindred dread
---

found you head-down beside
Ottis' bookstore
while looking for a crate.
you had a blooded eye socket
just wanting a friend.
bitch & cunt sharpied on
your one & only shirt
---

old guy of gusto
who sweated when he raved.
painted a phoenix he saw
& for the price of free
commissioned me for an oil daisy
for his Daisy.
bifocals & cane
refusing to tire in a retirement home.
been in love for 45 years.
truly passionate for life
---

incomparably sweet wives
from north dakota;
genuine marriage goals

First Contact

the boy alone
surrounded by
swaths of humandom
plethora of man;

solace only
in stellar masses.

driven to contacting
life outside
our biosphere.

four decades
& zero children;
he sent his message out
10X the speed of light
from his backshed.

four decades later
he received a message
in language not
made by lungs or tongues.

incomprehensible.

deemed senile
& riddled with dementia.

he didn't care for the prognosis.

<u>Broken Bronco</u>
Old bull Charlie
with sickle horns
& a rollercoaster
for a spine.

Would knock boots
off of their back
in 2 seconds flat.

Charlie The Unconquerable
they'd all call him.

Children awed &
adults oohed.

Even pros got weak in the knees
before they buckled in
to be bucked off.

Commercials for Broncos
used Charlie as a spokesbull bullhorn
of strength, of power.

Charlie knew he was confined
to this life
but he chose to make his prison
into spectacle,
his pain into the pain of
his captors.

He'd make them
Fear the heat that steamed
from his nostrils,

Marvel at his
Picasso paintbrush
of a tail
as he painted
opponents into pulp.

His handler Damion
was the only one who attended
the funeral.

His horns as
his tombstone

in the outskirts of El Paso.
They were found
in 3300 AD (After Detonations)
by the Greatest Genghis.

His left horn was the grip
of his 'unbreakable sword' and
right was hollowed into the horn
that howls for a new humanity to come
a new era of conquest
of radiation hardship
of grassland struggle
of unstable peace.

Charlie is now perfectly immortalized
in this museum a millennia later
thanks to the immense generosity
of The Genghis Goodness Society
. . .

Old bull Charlie
with sickle horns
& a rollercoaster
for a spine.

<u>The Brand New Brand</u>
iPhone nightlights
and samsungs
sing newborn
to sleep.

useless used for affection.

we lost the Oedipal love of
Mother Nature
when we could google milf
from our bedrooms;

when politicians could nuke
our species into extinction.

we lost our humanity
when humanitarianism
became just another commodity.

roses have become just
a cash-crop of love.

    "I am just what
     I want you to know.

    Better to sell yourself short
    than to be unsold and expired,"
claims my marketing professor.

Fluent Aphasia

Bloomed british flag
fireworks on the perry water
wet chilly water yo diggity
love kisses-es me.

All the short blurred lights.
Floorbound Rowan.
Fox in corner.

Flannel adorer Abby,
I love her more than any other.

I'm not a dog!!!
Gahhhhhhhh!
Getting the leg squeeze!

Leggys against shower-palm.

What is fountainhead
but what our segregated brains are.
Next level nose rub.

Mini.
Chess bound by spools
in snickering
dickering.
Flickering candles burning
yellow light
daffodil lemon lighght.
All the perfume
percussions
eye glaze cypress
aurora borealis .

damn God
callin me.

Phase 4 calm down.

Moose touch moose
tiny boy baby baby.

Shoreline shines

stronger than
brandy bursts
velvet upperfloor.

Lord adored in more than
a few pews.

Pewdiepie
the unpraised christ
reincarnated.

Natural disasters every day.
Murder in the word burns.

Vodka screwdriver
freshing plucked glass
in citric assets.

Love that pun
by love on ground.

Oh god lights
from east
end west beside me.
Up to the left.

Rekt Ralph.

Representative Tallyway
taken too much Twiddy money.

Where memories,
where happy
days come.

In unison.
a hidden union.

"Chairs of childhood;
scratches from my dad's belt
and peoples clothes.

Had them before Zachary.

Always
think of my cat
before my parents

got her.
Were her chairs.
Fur all over.

When she died,
another cat named rose."

Oh God
there is electricity
in my metal hands;
liquid ironworks.

Another broken lumber goddess.
Plywood jesus.
Artemis reincarnate.
Pelican warmth heating in chest.
Baked in a bakery.
East of Zachary.
Daiquiri dearth unearthed
in heathen smokestains
of Heath Ledger.
Cigarillo diaphara.
Constantine constant.
Ice chilled hands now.
Nepal mountain range.
Hardknocked knees
tweezers in seizures.
Paranoid.
Feeling humans behind me.
Eyesight farther in scope.
Reflection in air.
Lover kissing toesies.
Feet kissing.
Hear the cuteness
Gahhh!
All the words
flurry in widdle kicks.
Lungs perspiring grapeshot,
I am gone.

<u>On Ancestry</u>
in 6th grade
we watched
Schindler's List
& The Boy In
The Striped Pajamas.

even though
I had the hallmarks
of easy Nazi jokes
(Blonde Hair)
(Blue Eyes)

my classmates went
for Holocaust jokes
directed at
my skinny wrists
my sickly complexion
my starved look.

I wore hoodies
& long-sleeve flannels
well into spring
to avoid mockery.

this bullying gave me
a lot of my personality.

wasn't until freshman year
that I discovered a relative
died in a concentration camp.

makes me look back on those
jabs by classmates
& think that maybe I didn't
have it so bad

think that maybe humans today
were doing a lot better
than the previous century.

Starfish
and the urchin ocean of night
full of four-legged starfish
dizzying in splendor
in incandescent scent
in an afterglow of
lemon clouds,
tumultuous earth
singes browbeaten brows,
cuts down knees
like mowers shred orchids.
abysmal stares
of passerbys
pass by us all.
squandered time
time & time again.
dreams repressed
by our own doubt
own defeat

the forces against us
would pale in comparison
to the world
we allow ourselves
to deserve.

A Poem Dedicated To Andy Kaufman

swimming through hula-hoops
the bossman yells a yellow hello
the yelps of radar show subs on the horizon

juggernaut in space douse their ashtrays
in firework smoke

clams fall asleep on oyster beds

the feeding tube slips out
& another patient flatlines

grass grows only towards the street
& dogs love to lick up its shreds

midwives kiss their sons off to school
a brown paper bag tucked in an opaque backpack

of all the lands beneath the warming
wasteland; love, of my love, grows
more radiant every waking

kudos of karate master
goes a long way for kids

and the nunchucks were invented by
Benjamin Franklin in 1785

skipping stones to pass the time
passing notes to pass the time

pigeon-toed doves deliver letters
from far away,
they faceplant into
volcanic glass window sills

new zealand silt
soaks kiwis' feathered fluff;
but tangerine trees outlive them all

acorns are actually grenades
and leaves are laser guns
the squirrels are the combatants
and the time spent outside
hums our human tune with fun

gerrymandered jerrycans
for mother's uncle tim

porch light for the dean's list teen
out on a backseat car date

prognosis can't be right
surely a mistake has been made

rhinestone buckle beatings
if the cows produce only
black milk

cherokee cheeks red with christmas;
wrists slit with arrowheads
and glass over skype

cross-pendants bloom in from
pastoral pastures

traitors treat treaties with retreat

                        I miss Stewart

teen waiting in car
talking with a love he thinks
will leave before
the battery needs another charge

fathers grow old enough
to watch their sons abandon them

the human condition
a perfect hair conditioner

curlyfry eyes of crazed creation

the malts have melted in the stall

<u>Scalped</u>
     bricks of airliner tilapia
     hunking swivel trays;

beige ceramic mug
of watered-down joe;

     turbines humming hymns of
     a stricken atmosphere;

sushi-train of luggage;

     yellow taxis
     harbingers of
     sunny fog;

purple petticoat people
suede down indiscernible streets
in jutted cubist struts,
in limps of hacked lymph;

     nigh a nymph of stressed night
     bellied up on open-water
     below low-lying bridge
     flanked by riverbanks

sighs sighted by looky-loos
of a loser given up
given in;

     metallic birds wasping
     their airly penumbra
     no bigger than a slum;

     the lone freight train of Euphrates
     rollercoasting overhead;

the crumbling coliseums replaced
by gymnasiums,
by museums of amusement;

     sinks
     of sulphur bath-houses
     painted with white mold;

sons of treason
loiter around chalk outlines

of looted bodies,
a game of hopscotch
considered by all
suggested by none

bounty of flies
settle within the lines;

        syrup fills waffle squares
        of a cubicle breakfast;

    fireflies flicker
    greenlight neon
    before fainting;

trash-cans brimming to rim,
indifferent to bag or balloon;

        3rd floor of highrises,
      beachfront property by noon;

peninsulas made of pencils
of emptied penicillin
of civilian casualwear
of wearied garb
of turpentine & top-hats;

    sullen soil grunting
    in blooms of jellyfish-esque;

sapphic soak of a righteous unruly
shrinking the flannel &
staining blue jeans red;

    noirish ore origin unknown
    found swaddled in cement
    in melted maple
    marbled tile warped by warring;

cheap chapbooks filling in potholes;

    drummers are the new dreamers,
    hummers the new hammers;

yammering mothers of others
yiddish-ish in condescending speak;

      gars envy sunken gargoyle faces
      envisioning such monstrous jaws
      as their own;

fermented cactus brew
a delicacy;

waifish eat
crawfish & lemur-brain
etouffee;

      "from the blackberries of Berryman
      to the ash of Ashbery
      a poetic pigment
      dies America";

cars engraved with passing keys,
the midwives gunho on gumbo,
lockets of alabaster pills,
cereal bowl rice soup,
beatings of mikeys making the
kindest godfathers,
dragonflies lighter than argon,
Oregon trail now a railroad,
Mike Virgil with feet
planted between rails,
hydrants geysering majestic sewer,
biplanes spraypainting barley
with their best asbestos,
absinthe turning 80s synths
into sensation beyond (the limited)
Aristotelian 5;

    beckoned fear
    is a beacon
    is a Bacon
is a brokeback scoliosis ridge
of weathered angular boulders;

    gnats kiss
    subway-engines'
    shoveled cotton,
as morning commuters
scramble up some leftover Humpty Dumpty;

fawns tiptoe through creeks
with wobbly skeletal legs:

      a mojave brown
darkened like grandma's camper rug;

"*spiderwebbed phones*
more common than spiders;

"*libraries used only for*
book-burning rallies;

"*retinas clogged with tin;*

"*sci-fi the new syphilis;*

"*science the new sinus infection;*

"*nostalgia the new nostradamus;*

(sleep outlawed);"

to back home I fly in my
bathroom-stall pedestal

engine stalling on 737 at 736 AM

sudden splash landing

airlifted to naval barge

shipped back home wearing
beige cargo-shorts of the joe
who sat next to me.

The Last Hope Of Whitman Part 5

frat guys gawk at hawks nestled in a nest
while "**negross**" dissolve on a noose.

"*nostalgia the new nostradamus*"
says the man trying to sound deep.

algae festers on the alligator smile,
but our friendship never soiled
by garment galivants.

still young. maybe 5-6 decades left.
the days are becoming indiscernible.
blurred into one slog of long.

"need more caloric intake I take it"
jokes Dr.Charlie.

last time seeing Charlie.

next doctor will be for adults.

drinking now on weekends,

from the toilet half-naked
puking
Cane's & Able's chickens
along with potatoes
liquid & solid
into a tub.

celery stick sized canoes
funnel peanut butter &
dead ants to cleanse the tastebuddies.

    jellyfish plastic-bags carry home
    doggy-bags of bluebird bones.

pale adults padded in flotation
buoyant with sunscreen,
hitching my breath by foggy moonlight.

we see
river-going governors
kiss newborn anti-christs
from our
tibetan terraces

overlooking this well-furnished orleans;
whose drains clog
with gator toes & tourist teeth,
whose hearts weaken from grit and grits,
whose sun rises from the west bank.

<u>My Relative Relativism</u>
"what we think
about pink
due to
Rosa Winkel

bow to Bowie
the Pessoa of music

men dress in red dresses;
men who identify as women
dress in red dresses;
and nobody cares for a day

red means republican
blue means soyboy

colored a term
of disparagement amongst us
in the US,
but ok in the UK

queer a term viewed as
both empowering
and disrespectful here

news outlets tricked into
thinking the ok sign
is a KKK sign;
into thinking white milk is
the favorite drink of neo-nazis

gender is on a spectrum
that isn't visible within
any color of the rainbow

what is deemed
feminine masculine
maternal paternal
made by pattern making machines

all colors,
names, clothes,
jobs, thoughts,
are gender neutral
because gender stands
no taller than the neutral ground

biology sends more men into engineering
more women into physicians
more men into crab fishermen
more women into teachers

but the big five
isn't big brother

an individual in a free society
can accomplish nearly anything
if one wishes it, if one
pushes themselves endlessly

we don't call a robot in nursing she
a robot in accounting he

we are given bodies
and form our personality around it &
in unison with those around us

we are given intelligence
and form our (...)
(...)

we are given society (...)

R.I.P the spanish language."

"Yeah, but what if you're wrong?"

Anthro Apologist

it began with howls & grimaces
a smile in the water's surface

empathy neutered evolution

the trees thinned
and we find ourselves
on hindquarters;
find ourselves
walking
running
chasing down four-legged food

hoofprints and scratchings
become our first written language

markings on trees signalling
our existence to other sapiens

our first semi-permanent
voiceless hello

fire facilitates
a growing cortex

elders draw with fresh charcoal
knowledge in images
on dried pelts

stories of heroism become
religious because a community
of saviors keep the genetics thriving

witch doctors invoke divinity
for microorganisms are so small
they must be demonic
and the medicine is so small
it must be magic

deceit infected genetics
because one's life is worth
lying for and those receptive
to certain lies lived into adulthood

fashion fostered individuality
told stories

a lion tooth necklace said more
than spoken words

gossip birthed ethics

tribes grew
and grew tired of
the nomadic way of life

life grew from the land
when planted

weaponry turned on its own
and slavery dug canals in Indus dust

laws chiseled into stone chess-boards

language and math
propped up cities
kept a prospering ruled populous

the library of alexandria burned down

frail hands of monks blessed gutenberg

our words survive in servers,
vaults of a billion billion bits.

the library of congress will burn down.

our words survive in lunocentric orbits;
in satellites of a billion billion bits.

Memories

I close my eyes and eat my lips
as the poison spraypaints my face

I sit on shallow sand beside
the boat ramp and stay motionless
so that the minnows nibble on me

Sunscreen sticks to my skin
as I walk barefoot through the woods

Mosquitoes pant upon my belly
but my hands are faster than their wings

A horsefly finds me and its buzz
scares me back into the water
I kick beneath the surface
geysers of get outta here

I drive around on the blue 4-wheeler
and see other people I do not know
driving their 4-wheelers;
Red white and blue beings
hugging tight to one another
as they zip along the pathways

I play Mario Kart against some other kids
at the house of the family that
shares the land with my own

There's nobody the same age as me
and that kinda sucks since there's 40
other people here

I eat celery and drink coke and
walk around paths I shouldn't
to keep busy until the fireworks come

I talk with Papa Pete and he talks
the way I wish all old people talked

I find an attic at their place filled
with beautiful yellow dry foam goop

"The fireworks were nice this year,"
we would say on the drive back home.

Canal Street Now Just Another Unnamed Canal
the gardens bloom
catsup and satsumas

the kittens lick
the cement puddles
of sunwarmed cola syrup

the freshly painted docks
pyre with the distant petrol towers

the plasma TVs
rise and fall with plastic
in the estuary
like lava lamp bubbles

the shoeless kids float in
dumpster-doven fridges
and porcelain tubs

the dolphin fins suffice as
makeshift propeller blades

the superdome reclaims
the guinness world record
for world's largest cereal bowl

the retired deacons anchor their rafts
with jump rope
while illiterate children
use budless aux cords

the mothers curl their
creole hair
with telephone plugs

the whittled corks
of yellow wine bottles
and leftover newspaper
plug the leaks in the doors

the saints wear
onion ring halos

<u>Unrequited</u>
    Describe to me
    your love-life
    Ms. Hinzer

only ever the one.
only the one I wanted a
forever with.

year abroad
in bedlams of New Zealand
culticenter of Auckland

climate was rainbow
traffic-cones were sheep.

a professor
of geology,
her hair pronounced
the way bohemians
pronounce souffle
the way ostriches
lick ears of puppies.

I a TA
that year,

when Nigel offed himself
no longer owned a reason to return;

a return to vendor address,
none.

heavily considered an abode
in stereotypical
heaven/hell

made no difference;

nothingness seemed preferable.

tried bungee jumping,
a test run of sorts.

was numb on dumb
so was without wherewithal

stepped off perch
plummeted 108 meters
towards a river wrought with
    ships
in bottles
of yellow wine,
bifocals,
& jumpropes
knotted in her slushy blue.

step on gaseous ground
felt like a comet
coming for like,
T-Rex skeletons.

     for Nigel & Cynthia

     regret swept over me,
*"what was I doing
 this is the end"*

nothing to stop
sky rushing upward.

rubberband harnessed
secure around ankles
kicked in.

yanked away
from calming depths
of nothingness

flying into elation
elevation

     all I could see was
     my professor

     Dr. Dorine Peller

 Why her?

don't know,
don't know if
I'll ever know

some intangible levity to her;

a comforting heart.
in my time of need

days/nights hadn't a difference
within my shutters

I didn't care to eat
because it just meant having to
get out the bed to use the bathroom.

my bedside trashcan wreaked.

noshowing lectures,

little life
to respond back
to her
emails
texts
phone calls

she knocked
on my door
came in
at 8 PM;
door had been unlocked
for a few weeks.

she had me undress
the covers from my
barren body
spotted with malnutrition
& get into clothes;

gave the 1st hug in months.

she dragged me to a sushi joint
and had me try everything;

made me forget for a moment
my mental pain.

told me of her brother,
killed himself when she was 11.

did it with dad's pistol
while she was napping

in her own room.

her husband
has seizures.
had them doing his thesis
in Japan.
whenever the cherry blossoms' scent
pilfered his nostrils
he'd be unable to see
the world around him,
would become a hellish darkness
sieging his body.

she was once a schizophrenic
dealing with hallucinations,
conversations with people she knew;
it made her first
few years of undergrad
near impossible.
she was terrified
to start taking medication for it,
fearing it would make her less of herself,
fears instilled when young.

she thinks she'd have flunked
& killed herself in shame
without them.

she was a decade older than me.

a natural brunette
with skin tanned from field work

a New Zealand native that
grew up on Red Stag hills
grew up watching sheep marked blue
with a spraycan death sentence.

made my breath hitch
when unprepared.

hanging there above the river,
being lowered down to the boat
it clicked within that
        I
        was
        in

love

within every fiber optic
of my being
every ounce of my existence

    What happened
    when you confessed?

She was a kind-hearted soul
you know.

She invited me over to dinner
a few days after the bungee.

Introduced me to her husband
Norm.

He had a beckham-esque jawline,
brownish-blonde hair,
a bit of an unkempt beard,
& seemed to be everything
she could ever need in a spouse.

She had made mutton & rice for us.

They apparently had no children
because they feared inflicting
them with their own genetics.

She had her tubes tied
long before they tied the knot.

Their frankness, openness
& probably two glasses of yellow wine
gave me the courage
& recklessness
to propose polygamy.

They politely declined.

I wanted a forever with her
but I understood
that it would never happen.

She wasn't attracted to me
and I got the message---

    Then what?

A few months later
they offered me to be
a surrogate for them;
I declined & left
New Zealand shortly thereafter.

    Well Ms. Hinzer,
    I think today
    has been very
    helpful for me.
    Thank you.

    I'll see you tomorrow at 4.

PostMaloneModernism

this is poem

words and words
of meaning

/\/\oder/\/ poe/\/\
\/\/ords & \/\/ordz
saying thi/\/gs /\/EW \/\/AY!!!

+hisis p o s t m o d e r n pome
ings do//n""""t ha\\v b|||e
d-e_f-i_nle *ords 2wo

this is poem
tired of meta
of self-analysis
tired of saying nothing new
and twiddling thumbs
trying new ways to say
same words

this is poem of genuinity
from anonymous being
speaking just to be understood
speaking to understand others
speaking not to just hear
their own voice proclaim how
brilliant they be
for figuring out that it is near impossible
for them to be genuinely sincere for there's
always some underlying motivation

just ferris wheel with each seat
as a generation
reacting to previous and future

meaning has become interconnected
with meaninglessness

snake eating its own head
vacuum sucking itself clean
an echo amplifying in the abyssal

Sand

wheelchair could never
wheel through the beach

dreary (money chasing) man
would sometimes
till the courts
in an elephant sized
orange tractor

division///division
perhaps dividends,
perhaps vision,
as reason

man who replaced
my father killed himself

smackdab
in yacht-land
until katrina

smackdab
in suburban
thereafter

childhood sandpit
full of perpetually
pitted parties

divided &
none conquer

the sand soft on feet,
the ref-stands
crumbling monuments

bars no longer with those
arcade games that ate
my quarters

balls deflate
spines deflate
anger dissipates

ash indistinguishable in sand

Cross Country Along The Bible Belt

gun popped
& the hoard of gangly teens
galloped for the first few hundred yards
to avoid trampling.

long legs wearing red short-shorts
and blue compressions,

a 5 year old timex
velcroed sturdy.

5 years of summer training,
of winter migraines;

ran a Texas length, or
at the very least a Georgia.

sprinting the final stretch
like "The Saints Are Coming"
during football games
& I am 9 behind the bleachers.

a pinkerton face
& wheezing;

led through the ringer,
my number pulled
like cows losing yellow ear tags
right before becoming burgers.

another long bus trip back home.
another year as state runner-ups.

no PB, but at least there were
PBJs on ice in the cooler

<u>Virgil</u>
> *He like a rock in the sea unshaken*
> *stands his ground"*

against the approaching
freight-train.

> *It is easy to go down into Hell;*
> *night and day,*
> *the gates of dark Death stand wide;"*

Mike Virgil proclaims me savior
in the ambulance.

> *Myself acquainted with misfortune,*
> *I learn to help the unfortunate."*

Myself acquainted with suicidal thoughts,
I wasn't afraid to die
saving another seeking death.

> *Each of us bears his own Hell,"*

Mike bears his abandoned father and
his own attempted fatherly abandonment,
Mike's babymama Tiffanee bears
the burden of November 20th 2014,
Zaire will one day bear the guilt
of driving her father to attempt suicide
when only 2 weeks old.

Zatarain Rain
coffee mugs of
crawfish tails

a brew of satsuma water,
of zatarain rain

bricks of soft crackers
scoop up
the way mice dig graves
with rusty spoons

on collapsible tables,
newspapers fulla world
spread like an atlas &
consumed by the mountain
of crawdads boiled by
dad with
potato bags and
can-sized corn

brewed with
a squeeze of lime &
a belljar of
orange.

the marshland of harsh
the marshland of god
provides everything everything

Ballad Of A Dadaist
symphonic satiation

radio station static ticks
808 flicks
seismic riffs

weatherman born in the same
weathervanity as cronkite

"pick me out a pigmy jacket"
said the bigmy

dialect of the coke glass
spoken in shimmers
in shattered weaponry

stingray blankets
of backseat
origamied into the foot crevice

roadside blew reticent blur

windshield vision ledge
mopped by blinking wipers

hitchhikers look like bikers

hitting them is probably
what they want

slush black
skidding like kids skiing

orange jumpsuits jumping
the tractors;
cops getting lost in the maize

the brazilian radio station
clips in.

How Poignant
knives chiseled into shrimp rostrum
serrating telson eyelids

pinch the tail
break the armor
slide the meat out white

bristles of the peropods
clamping at invisible gulfweed

spanish teacher died
of lung cancer months ago
found out today

it's spanish time
it's spanish time
get into your places
it's spanish time
it's spanish time
bright and shiny faces

cotton creatures

cheating poorly on seasons

the cucaracha

learning different dances

paper mache cutouts

told us she was the voice
actress of Dora the explorer

mrs. smith also died

choked to death
on something
leaving behind her children

made a project on lightning
for her

only song with lightning in it
had Travolta smile

fingers flailing dont know
why i am even here anymore
the days blur too much and
i dont even know what blur means

that ego death bulllshit
go with the flow
till the grizzly gobbles
you up buttercup
dixie blows
blasting eardrums into a
garlic powder press

or something like that
i guess

i just don't know

An Alibi Conversation

"brown bag christmas presents."

"relaxation without taxation?!
what a quaint thought."

"we should break the yellow light
to keep the stop lights festive."

"Joe Rogan needs to work on Rogerian arguments."

"where's the reef mrs.wendy's ad lady?!!!"

"Sherlock Stockholm."

"I hear the fire hydrant is full of fire."

"You can dry rice with old Nokias"

"Love comes from within, hate comes from without."

"Does penguin pussy taste like fish?"

"I found a pocket knife made from an elk that
ate too much Swiss cheese underneath the cupboard."

"Kleptomaniacs keep stealing my heart."

"Do we hate cockroaches just because they have
the word roach in their name?"

"DAN HAS NO DNA! HE'S A WARLOCK!"

"I think hobos are children of Hobbes."

"You think wrong. 20 lashings!"

"I wish our teeth were mash-potato mashers"

"You think right. 200 lashings!"

The Last Hope Of Whitman Part 6

mastodon tusk encased, enshrined,
in a glassy waiting-room crypt.

elderly await bingo death;
just needa
B 82.

death by malnutritioned pills,
pillows without carbs or vitamin dream.

cars without steering wheels
drive us willingly into
democracy approved concentration camps.

"goodbye autonomy,
freedom has been automated,"
    says maurice,
"modern man is an ancestral invention
a foregone astral conclusion.

environmental determinism
determined everything.

our nurture was developed by nature.

the fish always drown in lakes of gold."
///////
feverdream of images
of whiskey glass bottle
sleek and modern font high-tall
brown sudsless,
images of food
of incoming coma.

perhaps an oracle of tomorrow:
Tailgating Day.

first refreshing cool wind of fall,
an uncommon commodity, as I catalog
dense tablets of cuneiform suicide notes
stacked two horses high.

clouds of cold snow new to
the winds of wintered alps
of phoney smoke-signals.

kraken cherry blossom tattoo
with blue and pale ethnicity
now barely even a memory.

an undying love built
on frankenstein neuroses
lasts long as rotting barbacoa.

time firebombs the asukara flowerbeds
into a one person petting zoo.

bookies don't read Art Of The Deal
& artists don't make money;
they manufacture sympathy & empathy.

light pollution causing a rise in insomnia,
in cricket carcasses.

needy in need,

loveless in love,

hopeless in happy.

text silence from me to her.
doing the same thing someone else did to me.

nilsson can only do so much for nihilists.

unfair fairgrounds tomorrow
with fraternal livestock,
Soros backed booze bingers,
earnen keep
with tiger stripes
with tie stolen from headmaster
with pension pockets
with kegger kegels of upkeep.

shame they don't remember things
that bring peace, calm;

busy scrutinizing actions
& inactions
forever always.

felt undeserving of love
thinking their existence

warrants less.

*"I can't hate someone I understand
which is why I only hate myself."*
I say to all seeking forgiveness.

once a young crybaby from lower school
always caring about others
over himself,
yet still always alone
walking wooden playground perimeter,
avoiding the mulch lava;
being avoided like the white plague.

now content with life,
fulfilled:

    working
    on frenchmen with a typewriter
    as a summer job,

    painting in dorm room,

    helping my future life
    with vet school applications,

    falling asleep besides another
    without fear of the future to come.

Part 3: Inhumane Nature

The Last Hope Of Whitman Part 7

> *survived years of wanting to kill myself,
> nearing 9 months of not wanting to die.*

gatling gutted at tailgate twilight
lightpost askewed,
cement pillow plateau of place-
holder me
down on seated tuckiss
kissing dirt
& dirt
wondering whether the wash would run over
my sunken representation.

sloshed typing to myself
in text messages   a
manifestation festival.
A mass communication communist of understanding
can't even stand.

sun beating me as grapes glush
into scented purple water.
Made with Christmas's feet,
the first miraculous
hounddog boozehound slumdog trillionaires.

war; the opium, unaware
of naval supernova.

tankard men sleep in tanks.

PTSD of past WW2: VIET drills
in genetics...
allergic to pussydom,

   we want pussydumb
says platoon plato.

the cures are unicycles & psychocillibin
but both are illegal.

dat smirk or grin illegal it's so good.

spy plane I spy from parade ground
perch tiger squander.
wandering wondering

whether this life
is worth living again.

planet perpendicular no bifocals needed.
eyesight fading already at this age.
     Natural soulection.
unnatural dissection.
Sects of frats of sorority sorts
in booty shorts: white sheets with blue ties
khaki killers.

roommate of my love
got roofied night before.
found passed out on campus grounds.
grounded for underage sloshed
by UNI nitwits.

psychology major Cynthia,
maybe Cindy, (cindered memories)
wishing to take advantage
of inebriated neanderthal
of unsound mind me.

told her I was happy and good;
she bugged off.

     "I contain multi-tools, not multitudes."

strung along by hands of love
staggering about to stadium-way,

reunion on grass with other highschool chaps
drunk wearing college pride.
some of em from other collegiates
yet they wear more pride than my
green flannel that
some rando complimented me on.
said it was   *"gucci."*
asked   *"what ya listening to?"*

said   *"music."*

stumbled off. found AC reprieve.

we walked through streets
without orchestral creatures.

feet felt like flinting obsidian
with each stumbling step.

saw ryan wearing a fake mustache
saw trashcan huggers vomit empty stomachs
saw dirty-blonde longhair drunk tryna start fights
tryna grab girls asses he collapses onto
saw adults the size of children
saw middle-schoolers pretending to be older
saw black dude with no arms up to his shoulders
saw my own knocked knees beneath a lightpost
saw grey and yellow steps of stadium

when walking to see uncle ron I
stopped in a portapotty to piss
a hot muggy place. was on the phone with my love
who was working on her vet school essay.
I think I went into some self-hate how the only
redeeming thing about me is (omitted)
she told me about our meme of great jawline
6 ft, and whatever else I wrote in bad prose.

I worry that she will have to witness me
be a masochist for art, (told me last night
that I am brilliant and don't need depression
to be creative)
experience hell
to have something worthwhile to describe,
that it'll hurt her as the years come
to see her partner hurt himself.

conscientious of alcoholism in my genetics;
addiction in my family members.
if I had started drinking when younger
likely would be dead or in AA.
didn't start drinking enough to get drunk
until I was happy with life; at peace.

wonder how future me will interpret it all.

wonder what clone grandchildren will think
when consuming my consumerist words.
this language.
these thoughts.

surely hatred &
for good reason.

maybe they'll be smarter than our
face's facade.
smarter than this honesty.

Discarded Newspaper On Charlottesville

vile sprung forth in Charlottesville
wearing linens :chanting blood and soil:
picketing with Tiki torches & sieg heiling
the salute of Germans
proclaiming to be US nationalists. claiming to be
for the south. for states rights. for coal
country. for white rights.
fascists and anti-fascists clash in brawls,
in vehicular rundowns. black smoke rises
into the clouds. *"the cotton-esque nimbus*
      shall surely rain snow upon idiots;
         their corpses numb red."
the kkk of the past existed because they viewed
themselves as powerful.
the kkk of today exists because they know they
are weakling larpers of the past.
escalation begets bigotry.
alt-right vs. actually-right.
violence breeds more violence.
silence/silencing breeds more violence.
maybe Roof will get
exactly what he desired.
maybe Kim or Don will
nuke a city or two.
maybe we will survive this
for we've survived much worse.
maybe volatile voices
will prefer peaceful discourse.
dismantling ideas instead of limbs.
or maybe we will always be tribal humans.
or maybe we will someday
escape the scapegoats & be we.

Run Away To The Runway

lipgloss
limelighted
in photolescent
flashes

a
flash in
the pang
for a
starving
beggared

skeletal
ribbing corset
perfect
for runway

starvation
harvested
to better sell
cotton
candy-colored
vests.

big dreams
of being
ICON.

the con of
being iconic;

a half-life
quicker than
love-lives.

livestock
for stock photos
for photoshop
classes

for shopping
brochures
of the
burger bourgeois.

grabbing
cash-grabs
in hopes
it'll last.

we gravitate
to self-hate.

wish to be
role-models
for people
that view only
hole-models.

pimp
ourselves
in service of
the mammalian gaze

an affirmation
of existence;
solipsism
is the lipgloss.

nothing but

gazelles
when cheetahs
stalk
their meat,

a Giselle
when paparazzi
stalk
their meat.

The Goes On

ovenlight left on
like static tv
snowing a blizzard of pixels

the heat goes on

the breeze thanks you

the remnants of romance
of a love that crippled sunlight
blinded darkness

a deity died

killed themselves
not for us
but for our adoration.

washboards perspire eyelashes
from towels.

bushels of seashells
tell of organic carcasses;
clamshell souls.

sugar pearls
sugarcoat the seafloor
of atlanta.

ostrich try to eat fruit
birthing from the ground,
the white succulent
of skeleton trees.

oxygen supplies depleted by king kong:
nitrogen swaddles babies of landlords.

unmanned menaces
wear men's faces.

warehouses of spoilt fruit.

heartachoo
guzzoontight

fuzzy moon out tonight
hitherto another withered rabbit foot
another diamond mudslide
another teepee torpedoed
another technical mustardpiece
another novelty nudity
another criminal kindness
another shedded overcoat
another nether of neanderthal desires
another suppression of neuroses
another indiscretion discrete as DesCartes
another origami monarch butterfly burnt
another strawberry milkshake
another same as it ever was
another penniless ventriloquist
another foolish fish
another landfill filled to capacity
another globalized city
another king mayor
another universal individual
another godly ant
another coral reefer madness
another delinquent who lost his linguistics
another marshland harsh
another beaten lesson
another shunning
another beaten displeasure
another adoration without an ounce of worth
another deity deadbeat
another public testimony
another test for money
another copied copout for cops
another scapegoats for sheep
another cape for us slightly evolved apes
another trivial atrocity in
another city
another country
another county
another dried up riverland
another endangered kingdom
another endorphin dosage
another book in a dazed day
another eggshell thin eyelid
another samurai eating buttered rye-bread
another beady-eyed bead chaser
another amalgamation of gametes
another plutocracy of hades

another golden era of arranged ayn rand
another atlas mugged
another at last uttered
another loves no one and his genes die
another howler monkey named beatnik
another isolation chamber of lunchtables
another marx with the mark of the best
another cain unable
another huey prolonged
another hue that's new between pink and brown
another crucifix affixed
another overdose over the moon
another tidal dali painting
another lukewarm worm
another pop-music pope
another surface-level face
another musing sung unheard
another squalor howl unheard
another anguish extinguished unheard
another weaponized democracy
another ballot bailout
another walking-stick used as chopsticks
another john wilkes kissing booth
another brothel of othello
another cartoon car
another vestibule of vestigial fashion
another quarter-pounder costing a pound
another flounder fleshed of fish
another hankering for worth
another self-imposed crippling
another children's game played alone
another carbon appetite
another trypanosomes in the crypt
another cellulite in light-beer
another nightyear
another adoption adaptation
another vagabond on bailbond
another ramen amen
another rummaged dumpsterdive
another divebar in the red
another parking-lot mountain
another lamppost tree
another artificial sunlight
another artificial friendship
another authentic fraud
another cronie economy
another flannel company named Mannel

another offspring of winter frozen
another offwhite reality
another offblack illusion
another free-will freed willy
another poet banned from libraries
another noah unknown
another misty sent to saudi
another denae denying campus
another personality of currency
another cryptocurrency pyramid scheme
another confident lie becoming real
another recycling plant named tree
another bad word association
another corporate repertoire
another bribed bride
another bought marriage
another iconic con man
another toppled chimney
another bell chime
another efemmeral
another concoction of cottonmouth
another sealed salacious pamphlet
another undisclosed sum of sunrise
another plaintiff stiff
another cyan coated cyanide
another magenta agent
another agent orange
another napalm nap
another deforestation station
another memory of a memorial
another time-honored tradition
another tomb of the known soldiers
another pointless cicada
another castro castrated
another magnetic polarity flipped
another scar in the ocean
another afternoon fling
another catapult swing
another fine-dining fine
another finish-line
another finnish chap
another happenstance stance that's wrong
another CAPITAL punishment
another gesture interpreted poorly
another capsized capitalism
another unsocial socialism
another commonplace communism

another another another
another whitewashed caucasian
another caucus bought
another diogenes died
another gg allin ginsberg
another persephone phoney
another popeye the tailor man
another eye-patch salesmen
another groomed groomsmen
another bachelord party
another bow to the sword party
another crowned kingdom
another protosaic salene
another gargantuan gained
another mongrel wronged
another zygote got
another cross-stitched sweater
another handmaiden foot-model
another grim pilgrim
another pill popped
another cervix serviced with a saw
another mutilation of mute mutts
another pavlovian love
another artery drooped like boar intestines
another fool's failing
another betting on bets
another beating of betas
another deadbeat
another can't beat that
another can beat that
another wealth-imposed depression
another rocket made of rocks
another currency with an inflation fetish
another riverboat captain without wheel
another compass broken
another impasse unpassable
another voyage of the age
another godless gold-rush
another adrenaline supply-line
another cry for help
another cry for hurt
another cry for end
another cry for happiness
another cry for prosperity
another cry for war
another another another

This Long Suffering

```
     downtrodden
     chopped      tree
strapped     shoulder-blades
scraping     blister
leper        lover;

deadly       inevitable
gods of      earth

Roman demagoguery:
a      vogue     rage.

nest of nails
castle on low,
air hung        silent
       amongst
     executioner,
unconscious          plateau.

peanut-gallery catches
     meager
     anguish         and agony
     of an Agamemnon      man
     an optimistic          mystic;

chatterings of turpentine cloth imprint
worm
across
aisles              of onlookers.
                       spear in rib
a harpoon in the glacial waters

egalitarian     heaven
on equal        -footing
with root       -winged men.

this                      descension,
utilitarian               suicide.
```

Terrorist Eating Burger King

went to Burger King
instead of Church's Chicken

maybe a whopper
maybe a coke icee
some thicker cut fries,
chicken fries
if available

daydreaming of his
electric-chair throne

The Stranger (Lame Title)

cockroach snuck into the corner
of my bathroom,
no toilet paper
so I used a wednesday newspaper, (so brave)

losing my eyesight
at a distance,
harder to read the slides
in the auditorium (so tragic)

bought some salsa the other day
and I think I will reward myself
whenever I get done
doing exercises (so tangential)

haven't done this since Cross Country
years ago (nice backstory bro)

crunches, planks, sit-ups
push-ups
the usual (thanks, really needed to know that)

submitted 6 poems to Kenyon Review,
would bet my left nostril
I get rejected (specific)

the poem they picked last time
was horrid (ironic from you)

suppose I just
submit to them off of
name recognition (and never reading journals)

some guy pestered me into it
with his posts on instagram (that's pathetic)
I think he cares more about publishing
in journals than I do (well yeah, he's a publisher)

there is a manuscript contest for poetry
the "2018 Walt Whitman Award" will be given
to the winner along with publication (so meta)

I know the $35 dollar fee to submit
is a bloody gamble
but $5000 dollars

and 6 weeks in Italy honestly
ain't too bad (yep, Italy sure is a place)

luckily all the books
I had self-published in the past
didn't have an ISBN (wrong)

so I qualify for it,
I think. I hope. (you do not)

won't find out about the rejection
until April 30th, 2018 (you never submit)

they'll probably think
I had the title of this book be
"The Last Hope Of Whitman"
to schmooze them up (you changed the title)

whenever I submit,
I am gonna have to edit out
any instance that I use the name James
or Jim or White or whatever name I go by (failed)

anonymous selection process
they say (much needed info)

probably them just not wanting to be
accused of favoring one race or gender
over another (so socially hip yo)

so much for a deprecating line about
The King James Bible (ok, honestly kinda clever)

will probably include this poem
in the version that actually gets published (yep)

likely by myself on Amazon again, (yep)
or maybe if I am lucky
by some local publisher
that my former teacher
gets me in contact with (nope)

I think nobody wants to read about
not getting published (you are right)
but then again maybe they do (they don't)
maybe they want genuine honesty out of me
genuine failings that make me more real (meh...)

tell them how the place I did stand-up at
shut down and is now
a philly-cheese steak restaurant (kinda funny)

how I hate myself for not being as close
with my family (you should do better then)

how I struggle to write about the deaths
of people I loved because I always just feel
like I am exploiting their deaths;
dishonoring them (then maybe write better)

how I wanted to die daily for years (we all do)

how I am annoyed at myself for fearing
to take medication for it
fearing I would
lose my ability to write (that's pretty dumb yo)

how I am glad I never took medication
because I am at a sustained time in life
of immense peace and calm (you got lucky)

REDACTED (Jesus. I am sorry for that)

how the last hunts I went on with my dad
were more so for him and that I really
no longer got any joy
from killing (exploiting fatherly tropes)

how I feel shame when I don't give
money to homeless men at stoplights
after I make a 100 dollars doing
typewriter poetry (that's pretty scummy)

how my previous love
told me never to write about her (understandable)

how I obsess too much over what is
the real me, what is the genuine me,
what is just a character that I play
in hopes people like me
people enjoy me (don't we know it)

how my wrists are literally twigs

and maybe I have just been lying to myself
about my fast metabolism
when I eat usually only 2 meals a day
along with snacks here and there (you are healthy)

don't even know if I have had
2000 calories
in a single day
in my 20 years of life (you have you twat)

how I'm 6ft and 124 pounds. (and still growing)

how I have broken 130
once in my life (you probably are 132 right now)
(checked a month later. 132 exactly. god i'm good)

how I am fucking on the verge of
breaking down right now in sobbings
in fucking shame of my body
that I know some would kill for
some have killed themselves
for not having (yep, everyone hates their bodies)

how I think I am healthy and active
but I am not sure if my freshman 15 will
ever kick in (probably junior year)

I have had a bowl of cheerios,
two peanut butter sandwiches so far today
and that was 3 hours ago,
it's 6:15 PM right now. (dude chill, you were
just down that day and not hungry)

Sure I am hankering for a burrito
but I need to eat more
I need to gain weight. (you are fine)

my feet are cold because roommate
put conditioner down to 69,
gonna put socks on
and go get some food now (good idea)

shit like this is why I hate
being genuine (same)
so much easier to live
when you don't
think about it (still thinking on that)

I don't think I am going to submit
to the Walt Whitman Award. (good call)

Forgotten History

atop marble mountains,
decked in tangerine dyed cloth.

Kholoogin's goons march
through dense Mongolian forests,

booting up bottlenecking, winding flights;
ascending to ascetics.

canonfire outmatches Pāli canon;
their razors only good for suicide.

the purges sweep
like a broom of strawberries
like rose mountain initiatives.

a calmness haunts the cruel
carrying out the kulling.

in the riverways
bhikkhu bits meld with unplucked gold.

orange robes burn
& there's no grandchildren to mourn.

The Bay of Bayonets

molotovs lobbed into log-cabins,
teargas vaping in maternity wards,
prison-bars made of rusting bayonets,

mermaids soaking in ponds of
melted M&Ms,
the Army Corps of Engineers
pump the ponds dry;

Ariel gasping for air;
for cumulonimbus to swim in

children buy black gumballs
mounded in astronaut helmets
with 2 bitcoins

the stingy-sweat of
sweatshops sold
at a discount
in plastic bottles.

one day soon
unmanned tanks will be
powered by solar-panels,

we aren't ready.

Quarter Million Quarantined

fingernails plucked
like petals

ponytails lopped off;
shaven to the skull

nettypotted mucus

brows and lashes naired away

another nuclear holiday;

skies molding with
mushroom clouds
and oil rain

as winter comes
the glowing red and green survivors
wish they were

nuked into naked shadows
into imprints of principle
into winners of the winter

"There Can Be No Poetry After The Holocaust"

Ashkenazi ashing;

windshield wipers
tick tock the grey
the way grandfuhrer clocks
wipe themselves clean

adults with 29 teeth
huddled on the passing
train conveyor belt
sing songs of agnosticism
while pushing
and shoving in
a mosh pit of pity

Auschwitz ashing;

the steam engine chugs
it's metallic limbs onward
leaving behind those clouding
smokestacks of grisled grey

a few hundred kilometers away
the horn blows with
the music of air-raid sirens
for two red Volkswagens
stalled out on the tracks

Wandering Thoughts

earthworm writhing
in the middle of a parking lot
during a summer day

the eulogy cards you
hold onto in a metal box filled with
the only 5 photos you have of them

the bedside trash can

something I keep
to myself late at night when I pray
to things I stopped believing in

something we
wish we had less and more of

the grass regrown

the everything
for those that made
the right choices

The Last Hope Of Whitman Part 8

football game chats about chattanooga players
with rugby gal.
first quarter finishes after an hour of play.
gotta get them advert $$$.
still wonder why I desire this as my job.
selling goods, brands, products.
products that likely are killing us.

even escape is confinement.

baggage comes superglued
to our middle fingers.

there's no Jonah to pull,
no escape from humidity.

the meat and oil is good
for just a generation or 2.

Kittyhawks
turned us into hawks;

weak thumbs on big red buttons.

with box-cutters,
scaffolding folded
& elevators
sunk;

those baking
chose suicide
over imperial burns.

carcinogens coat
lungs,

yellow coats limp
in ash.

people of sanded villas
fear clear skies
fear dronestrikes
with 90% civilian
to 10% combatant ratio

fear that war
will never cease in ceasefire
fear that freshwater will dry up

fear me
fear whoever I vote for
fear my children unborn
fear my accent
even when I say I want you to live, love.

to be American;
a charlatan, a creep, a fraud,
a huckster.
one justifies slaughter
claiming eye for an eye,

more like an eye for an eye
      of a hurricane.

no armistice
only arming both sides
& reaping the red solstice,
reaping the opium,
mining the fallout glass,
drilling through the hourglass for oil;
a drying well of time.

congealed blood the new quicksand.

      merchant ships
      march & chant
"We Are Rich We Are Reichtious!"

Robert E. Lee
could have
been president
had he chosen the north.

Wankrupt

folks steal a pack of tortilla wraps
in hopes of being fed for five years

bankers scam folks out of 30 billion &
get 15 months if they get anything at all

    Hammurabi would take their hand
while America gives them a helping hand

       a bridge of rotten wood

       a shining landfill on a hill

       an anthill of piss

the music of songbirds sings sideways
       &
       throats
       perspire
       carbon
       monoxide

fever dreams of happytrails and chemtrails
   keep us on the rails of ruling law

   crime and punishment
now crime and profit
   law and order
half the time
just imprisonment of political enemies

       rockabilly abilities
        & wannabe charisma
   will keep the cruel unaccountable
as long as their accounts are stuffed
with dat beautiful bribery

blessed be the polevaulters of culthood
aints of sainthood
& hoodlums of rainbow collar work

<u>In Indonesia</u>

chinamen & communists
hung by a wire;
the man who wears
blue jeans
pulling the string.

gangsters of government
threatening the monger;
the shop-owner,

their money shoved
into pastel envelopes
& blown on blow
of every variety.

Pancasila youth
3 million strong
"3 Million Forever"

Yapto in tiger striped garb
sings into the microphone
resonant sonnets
for his tiger striped army.

The *"thick book
with all their names"*
owned by the
St.Peter of Hell;

feared by all,

for anyone can be
a communist,

an enemy of the
state.

"state your name"
he says to the pregnant mother,

"state your unborns name"

Morality Of The Story

> *"did they not know
> how truly terrible
> they were?"*

our descendants will ask
in class.

> "they ate slaughtered
> animals; how barbaric."

they will pat themselves
on the back for how civilized
they truly are;

not realizing that learned morality
often is dictated by technology
history & economic forces.

> "how could they be so cruel
> as to not let these animals live;
> to experience existence if
> only for a moment?"

their own descendants will say of them
after the great cattle extinction.

Khmer Rouge

from Baton Rouge
I read of Khmer Rouge;

another atrocity
in another country.

the Cambodian man Akira
defuses landmines
he planted in 3 armies
as a child
the way my mother
pulls weeds in her garden.

when there was no food,
foraging to survive
was a prison sentence
which was
a death sentence.

men & women
die in Yemen
yesterday & today,

my taxes backing
the bullets used.

so too will this devastation
be forgotten;
never taught in schools,

found only under the cities
built on cemeteries.

Jellyfish In The Tank

of pink outstretch
limp-armed seaweed

afterbirth
deformity.

children
clutching coins of white candy;
stench of pinched picnic.

chloroform formless;
feldspar tar.

    "grandpa died
    on bicycle day."

whale-sized walls torn down
for something new

aluminum cup
of living wage
and an emptied vessel.

Help Help Help Help me...
have you all none to give? please.

not so sure
about too much.

IV bags of clear
cleared away like grocery bags;

cotton-candy skies care only
for kites and kittens discarded
to the green dumpster.

Sunshine bleaches this glass town.

Spinedrift

drenched green sponge
birthplace of bubbles

an omnivore
of skillet scabs
breakfast barnacles

hyenas raccoon their noses
down garbage disposals

snoots looting
chicken cartilage
& lunch upchuck

pawed faucet still sputtering
spickets of aquifer

an ever soaking sponge

foam froths
within that
casket of a
bunker

unearthing, levitating
a cement sarcophagus

a barm container
of little laughters
barricaded by the breath
of dead wind
and lover thicket

Gulag

old men eat snowballs from their beards
on the distant porch,

> *it's 30 below*
> *but global warming*
> *is coming any day*

they say.

> *the end of 10 years;*
>
> *it's coming any day*

I say.

doctor says
> *your fevers 103*
> *luckily it'll keep*
> *you warm;*

guard says
> *if you try & run*
> *I won't shoot*
> *because my gun*
> *is empty*
> *& upper-ups say*
>> *frostbite is much*
>> *crueler;*
>> *so let them freeze*
>> *in freedom.*

I'm told
> *we are 70% water*
> *so I am not that far*
> *from snow*

squad leader says
> *your water better*
> *not snow on me*

Ivan says
> *please don't forget me*
> *when gone*

I say
> *you'll be free*
> *any day*

nobody risks
purple hands
just to pray

Drones

white wings
invisible in
clouds;

hellfire
turns dunes
into glass.

children
preserved
the way
mammoths are
immortalized
in tundra ice.

camels evolve
their hooves
into glass-skates.

caravans carry
bountiful opium
over charred
carcasses,

those maimed now
opulent with opioids
bought at a discount.

Genital Mutilation

crotches
of newborns
crippled
by midwives
who can't
find their own clits

as is tradition

Terrabytopia

humanity must achieve immortality
otherwise the changes needed to allow
for a healthy world will only
be exacerbated by salesmen that
don't have or don't care about
their grandchildren

mountains of trash
and cities of smog
will become romanticized
by the greatest poets turned
propagandists

those with large voices will tell you
speaking or writing is pointless
for you are only a morsel in the
terrabytopia

they will say the ripple effect
ripened into rot long ago

universal consumer income stipends
lended out into everyone's
blockchain skull parameters

consuming surplus and disposing of excess
will be the only occupations post-scarcity

despotic automation will bring
a peaceful paradise like no other

resistance is futility in emotion
once game-changers become interchangeable

nature vs nurture
now only neural networks

we were banished from eden at the discovery
of our nudity
we will enter eternity with the genetic help
of the naked mole rat

supercomputers will simulate googlefold of itself
until it can simulate triple helix sequences
of every universal possibility

simulate universes
of every potentiality of life

when we realize this is a simulation
we will treat the universe like a videogame

customizing our aesthetics with genetics

uploading consciousness into our characters.

"every big bang occurs within a black hole

the universe is a self-replicating rock
of cosmic mitosis jiving in the riverbed of 4th,"
the 23rd century scientists will say.

the qubit compactor will spit out,
"time is the 1st dimension,"
but we will be too timeless to care;

caring will be left to the algorithms.

feelings of inferiority that once created
that which was supreme
replaced with simple alterings

but now creation is created for cyclical sake.

when our present day systems promote
individuality so unabashedly
ego-death and love become the greatest
of lusts

"love is a technology
corrupted by those
seeking self-gratification"

"love is a flexible evolving enslavement"

is what I would say before I found love

before I realized
that the hearts of past beloved
were bulbous hookworms.

from tinder blossoms tender embrace

of warmth and future.

choking on the chakra twig hauntings
that brewed one's bright essence
leaves the gardenia garden asphyxiating
within the white picket fence of rib.

from self-destruction comes
the indistinguishable selfish and selfless
and an end that doesn't
correspond with its start.

absurdism is the lovechild of purpose.

sophistry is the loveparent of relativism.

plato only ever knew platonic love.

your blue is my red.

my south pole is your north.

your jack in the box tastes like trash.

Telephone-Wire Jump-Rope

These freckles are recording me
seeing what all I do

I'd wear a cloak but then
they'd just make me perspire

The device in my tear ducts
is controlling my mind to write out
every thought it has

Confess it all

I've been lied to
about the cure

forgiveness is avert me

<u>The Color Black</u>
Cyan candy skulls
are sold for $2.99
from divorced vendors
in cemeteries

Teens suck upon them
till their inner cheeks
& teeth are coated
in an ocean of sugar

The date of
The Day Of The Dead
overlaps with
my sister's birthday.

Yellow buds of tickseed
munched upon, roots & all,
by a doe and her twins

Perched in a crows nest
I gaze at their hearts
tucked behind their front legs
with a scope dad got me

I've wounded too many mothers
to squeeze.

Magenta cardinals sing songs
of serenity to the magpies
drowning with bits of small plastic
in the peppermint colored marsh

The quarried mud road back to the barge
full of buck tracks;
the treeline crust whittled by fresh scrapes
& nared naked by winter

Dad skinned the rabbit while I fished.
I slipped it into a double body-bag of black Glad.
On the drive home, he complimented my headshot
& said that the meat all looked good.

A.P.O.L.O.G.Y.
I. remember. joking. with. friends.
about. my. honors. english. teacher.

the. "what. ifs." of. a. "birth. defect."
the. "how. fucked. up." of. a. "stillborn."

.I .was .so .glad .that .she'd .be .absent
.for .a .quarter .taking .care .of .her .baby

.She .was .the .hardest .teacher .I .ever .had
.& .I .felt .she .hated .me ".because .I .was .a .guy..."

She.alone.made.me.desire.Genuinely.Dying.
more.than.any.other.stranger;

When I, rarely prayed. I prayed, that
she. Would just, get fired.

Her son died and she took a semester off.

During 11th and 12th grade we would
occasionally chat in the hallway about comedians.

I'm sorry.

The Last Hope Of Whitman Part 9

temporary stars dwindle
above muddy beaches.

mangroves untouched by man;
yet still
boiled by us
salted by us
& uneaten.

estuary salvations salinated
into brackish,
into blacked with salt.

mother mangrove regrets
granting man life,
breathing out that which
sustains an unending maiming
of motherland by those
she cherished unconditionally
in the bountiful harvests of breathing
in glassless milk-bottles of uncarbonated.

our mangrove mama,
she's watched us grow from minnows
into marsupials
into mammalians
into beasts dwelling outside the food-chain;
littering metallic corpses onto garbage islands.

knees of our mothers curve down into
deadly soot of steamboat exhaust
of burnt aged-algae,

they pray into the core mantle,
where latitude meets longitude.

they cry into the tectonic reaches;
exhaling exhalations of pleads
via neural root begging as
magmatic pockets cigarette their lifelines.

mother mangrove prays
to the heartbeat of terra
with terror in her
xylem lips &

spanish moss tongue. praying
for the end of this demon-child run amok.
mocking that which nurtured them
making that which natured them into deforestation
as though it was second-nature
as though city was first-nature
as though grey cement could grow blooms of buds
pillars of grass
towering oaks;
the way her fertile could.

the mangrove knows
man can't be killed
no matter the plague,

for they have supreme adaptability,
imperial cooperation.

mother mangrove withers;
crying saltwater
into the missing Mississippi.

a Louisiana sunset strikes the marshland gold,
the cityscape glows in orange heavenly.

mother mangrove dries into driftwood
& is carried out to gulf.
sent from coastline to receding coastline
until landing
upon the land of the rising sun
where she became the last bonsai tree
crafted with natural wood;

some last hope of Whitman.

Made in the USA
Middletown, DE
27 May 2018